For Sharon
from your now cultured husband!

All best,
Sara Berkeley
Armagh
27 July 15

Gallery Books
Editor Peter Fallon
WHAT JUST HAPPENED

Sara Berkeley Tolchin

WHAT JUST HAPPENED

Gallery Books

What Just Happened
is first published
simultaneously in paperback
and in a clothbound edition
on 30 July 2015.

The Gallery Press
Loughcrew
Oldcastle
County Meath
Ireland

www.gallerypress.com

*All rights reserved. For permission
to reprint or broadcast these poems,
write to The Gallery Press.*

© Sara Berkeley Tolchin 2015

ISBN 978 1 85235 645 3 *paperback*
    978 1 85235 646 0 *clothbound*

A CIP catalogue record for this book
is available from the British Library.

What Just Happened receives financial assistance
from the Arts Council.

Contents

Cracking Open *page* 11
If I Met You Now 12
Sitting with the Art 13
Crown of Vines 14
Outliers 15
Sun and Standing Still 16
Things that Keep Me Awake 17
King Tide 18
What We Seek 20
Swan Geese 22
Sailing 24
Barn's Burned Down 26
Gone Driving 28
O Holy Life 30
Snapshot 31
South Beach 32
St Laurence's Ward 34
Sweet Creek Corner 35
Fall Back 36
Burrow Beach 38
The Hour 39
Delta 7123 40
Shutdown 42
Dahlias 44
When We Got Home from Paradise 46
Bluebellies 47
The Last Word 48
On Not Scattering Michael's Ashes in Death Valley 50
Sleep Train 52
Emergency Chocolate 55
Ceanothus Celestial Blue 56
What It's All For 57
What Just Happened? 58
Ice Diamond 59
Universal Laws 60
Ashes, Phoenix 61

Big Dry 62
Famine Cottages 64
Coyotes 66

for Connie
and *for* Niamh

Cracking Open

See these lines —
laughter wrought them
carelessly at the corners of my eyes.

Brown skin.
Sun bore down.
Damage, some say. I say skin memory —

that wicker couch
with the soft red pillows on the porch,
noon ablaze with the songs of bees;

late afternoon's
generous abundance:
seven different types of light;

hummingbirds
flickering by the bottlebrush,
then flying off, wings a blur, into the future.

Should I grow older
and the light more distant,
small animals hiding under the skirts of evening,

I'd like my heart
to be without conditions,
to crack each day a little more open.

If I Met You Now

If I met you now and you asked me
how I was going, I would say this:
very far and very fast.
Poems crowd me, sometimes
five to a page. Money burns a hole.
All caution aside, I'm running
with the wind aft and the sheets
eased out. This is no close-hauled tack
but a full sail into the eyes of the weather.
The heart without compass.
The journey without a map.

And if you accepted that
I would have to add:
I need to sail alone. Sometimes
I look from shore to shore,
the difference between twenty-eight
and forty-four; my world tips up
and they come pouring out of me,
songs I could never have sung back then.
The headway I'm making now
with a true wind, it's the answer
to a certain call among girls.

Sitting with the Art

On this happy afternoon — no accounting
for the light, the space, the storm
of paper planes out of a perfect sky,
the clouds hanging back because
they haven't the heart — I'm sitting with the art
at the Spring Art Show, watching over
the watercolours and the oils,
the chalk pastels and the salvaged materials.
They're nodding together in twos and threes,
expectant of admirers, and watching over me
as I take out my assorted pencils, theodolite,
compass and sextant, and prepare
to be the draughtsman of my life.

You need a ground plan, a roughcast draft
to be the inventor of something
as labyrinthine as a life. You need vaults
and cornices. You need straight lines
where there cannot be straight lines.
You need proofs, and when they're ready
you need to tear them up and start again.

Crown of Vines

Now and then life needs a new page
opened flat out and white with a slight crack
of the spine as though to show for a moment age
is an earned reward, a shared joke, a consolation.

If you can't write just yet put the pen down
and take up a straw, a spear, a flower.
It doesn't matter what vines you use to weave your crown;
it will fit, no matter. You're the bearer of the rings,

the dancer of your dreams, you play
the music that makes the neighbours throw their windows wide
and smile and maybe one to the other say:
Can you hear it? Shall we dance too today?

Outliers

We met on the way back down,
the show was over, they were giving the tickets back.
Blundering round our living room,
the elephant was knocking photos off the walls,
shaking the pins loose.

He had an oversize shadow.
The way love overlays the blueprints of our lives
disrupting the heart's own blood supply,
the coronary arteries bleeding out,
you would think we'd know not to pass by here again.

The locus of all pain
has been pinpointed somewhere between 2 and 3 a.m.,
the wellspring of tears
hides in a seahorse store of memories
curled up deep in the brain's hold.

No more secrets.
Look at us now, outliers in our own town,
there's nobody living in our living room,
the cups hang empty on their hooks,
glass underfoot.

But we're a late loss species.
Shouldn't we have a few thousand more rainy afternoons
to play with? Time to stand
and soak in the scent of lilacs by the rain barrels
under our eaves; time to slip a hand

into a hand, and feel
the way love sends its shafts of light late and at an angle
showing up the motes and all the busy air,
and how the thunder's always there
lying low beneath the sunlit evenings.

Sun and Standing Still

I didn't start out alone, but in formation,
dispersal, wind over wing,

me and my brothers, downflow behind us,
uplift in the wide arc of the distal feathers,

sun for compass. When the wind shed off the bird
in front and beneath us the shear flow of the air

changed its expressions, its knowledge of us,
the rightness of flight threw down its scarlet cloak

for us, caged birds
altered their flight paths

as we shifted course — their wild cousins
flying into the shortest light

towards that strange and beautiful place
where the sun stands still and the earth rests

for a moment on her axis, stilled from turning.
But sometimes in the exhausted dawn

a heavier bird falls, spiralling down
wing over wind in the first unforgiving

wash from the east, a flat spin, a stagger
onto an empty beach. Trash can. Sun. Standing still.

Things that Keep Me Awake

That pin
dropping as the cat pads across the kitchen floor,
her paw on the cat door. I don't even know
why I'm frightened any more, my thoughts
clanking round the junkyard of my brain,
spare parts stacked high — a dollar to haul them away.

It's 3:14. Night turns over with a sleep sigh
taking my share of the blankets.
The shirt-tail of a dream flutters by.
Canada geese. Not that I can hear them,
just that somewhere, out of the clear blue,
their low, slow, mournful honking
threads its way through the sun's yellow eye.

I sit up in the powerful dark,
the unmanned silence of space
bears down on me. So this is how it works:
neither slow nor fast, time stretches
from end to end of my life, neither
too long nor too short. Everything in between
is a vast expanse of ice, dark young nilas,
brilliant in the sunlight.

Every morning I step out on it again,
just enough weight to make it groan,
the plates raft over one another.
Sometimes I have to leave myself behind,
my thin spirit takes to the floes,
crossing with ease; and there are nights
I just have to lie back down at the blue edge
and hope to fall.

King Tide

Change is coming up
like the ice floes breaking off,
exploding into the high air.

I'm wearing a smile and it holds
the tiny doors in my heart
shut.

Sea change coming, a tidal thing, lunar,
that boat I didn't want to rock
gone belly up,

that prize I didn't want to lose,
under the glare of my sights,
bloodless, listless,

no longer a presence
in my inner life.
I wrote love

out of the script, eager to sail
alone with my music
and my thoughts.

Now this king tide
washes the boat ashore. I need
to swim out

from under, get some air, take stock.
Lay bare the heart.
This is where

I could hold or let fall,
hold or let fall
everything dear

and familiar. Time to feel
it all, let rise to the surface
what will

and gather it in both hands
so the pieces tremble
together.

What We Seek

We were dancing when the ground opened up,
the sky opened up, the world was cold space,
the sun slipped into the sea.

We were singing when the wind came up
and with it the trees — they rose in the air,
there were limbs down everywhere.

Halfway across the distance between me and you
a wall came up. You searched for a door,
a way through.

On my side I rallied, I found joy,
sparked it up from two sticks.
I discovered my words were words of burning.

They caught from one another
the fire of longing, of despair,
they sent their flames far up into the air.

I risked their spreading, I let them;
it was heady, crossing early and quickly
from silent fear to conflagration.

Thus was I deep into oration when the wall
fell. Suddenly tired of all the conjuring
I watched the flames get sucked into the sand.

It was dark when I began to climb,
hand over hand,
the sea below, pacing back and forth.

A blue moon barely lit my path,
the birds wheeled, ready,
salt stung my eyes.

I reached the peak,
insatiable hunger, unquenchable thirst.
Knowing I was not the first

to consider launching myself
from such a height
I closed my eyes, felt for true north,

the secret heart of all things,
and willed the red glimmer
of dawn to the tips of my wings.

Swan Geese

The days blur,
passed like cards from hand to hand;
it seems we're getting older.
Most nights are broken
but the mornings mend them.
Spring marches gamely on,
all the Easter colours raining down.
I'm trying to savour
every astonishing elusive moment.
To work at all
I have to be ruthless,
stuff time in a box with a lid and a lock,
let morning unfurl at her leisure.
Sure, I have to keep the tools
handy, but the real test comes
when two geese
fly honking over the hot cars
in the Target parking lot.
I'm squinting up at the sky
with no words to convey
the haunting evocative sound
they put out, nor the tumbling
card house memories they stir,
and who cares anyway
what mad jumble the past has to show
for itself? The geese are gone,
they skidded down in the saltmarsh
behind Jennie Low's. Perhaps
they have a brood of young
clamouring for worms, centipedes,
whatever it is that swan geese
eat. Something should arise
from their regal passage over
the cheap jewellery of Vintage Oaks

mall and parking emporium,
even if it's only this.

Sailing

I'm in a place where much hurt comes to rest,
a confluence of pain and rapture,
laughter and despair.
Hunger is acknowledged here,
loss hangs in the air,
grief is recognized, renewed.

The broken come here, endure
blinding light, engulfing dark.
This is a house of ill luck
built upon hope, layer above layer;
in this house, let the heart
incline toward kindness.

The people who stay here
sleep the sleep of those
who go on losing and losing;
they come empty-handed,
flung out of the orbit of their lives,
wrung free of ego,

drained of their insatiable self love.
I witness the ills that they endure
and when I mourn for them
all the old sorrows rise like water;
a cello joins the piano solo
in the house of their tomorrows.

Midday, I sit out on the hot bridge,
the frogs are in concert in the creek,
at ease; small miracles of heat
rise off the wood,
the planet runs on and on
with her disease

but I feel that something good
has been promised here,
something bigger than anybody
planned. After work
I sit a while in my car
before I put it into gear

and drive out beyond the daycare centre
and community church, far
past the tidal pull of all my patients'
sorrow, tugging at the ropes
of the small vessel I will sail
back to them tomorrow.

Barn's Burned Down

Barn's burned down —
Now I can see the moon.
            — Mizuta Masahide

I want to talk about Joe,
four days gone now. What to write?
Not about the death, there was just too much

of that, nor about the eerie hush
that followed the catastrophe,
the shaken nurses who had brought him

temporarily back. I want to talk
about the plum trees he's not here to see,
the tiny leaves and the shining

of the white blooms and the bees'
secrets they will carry back to the hive
just as they did on the last days he was

alive, early Spring such a heartbreaking
time to leave — shouldn't we all die
with the falling of the days,

towards the shortest light, and not at the moment
Nature flutters on the brink, tears in her eyes,
ready to break out in her tremulous aria?

I want to talk about how I loved
to make Joe smile. Rare,
grim little smiles, but I loved drawing them out of him.

On his last day he wanted to lift weights.
I joked he could help me with my nursing notes.
He smiled. Now and then

he would grab my arm as I gave him
what I called elixir of oxycodone for his pain.
Appreciation from someone who can no longer

speak is better than words
in any language, anywhere.
His last hours were hidden from me

but I was there for his last day.
None of us knows, do we? And yet
I wonder if the sudden lightening

of his spirits was a sign. Maybe he
already knew who he was meeting
in the faraway town. Whether or not:

I want to write about the two small birds
that flew in through the propped open door
while the medics were busy with CPR.

They flew around high up in the great room
most of that day, stopping only to gaze
longingly out the windows at the glassed-off world.

Eventually we set one free. The other
stayed in the rafters till late afternoon,
then flew down and directly into Joe's room.

We released him too. Free at last,
how he must have exulted in his flight
up and on up into the welcoming light.

Gone Driving

Fall now, no escaping.
First rain broke the spell,
the hot dry promise
broken by the downpour
and the next day's damp loamy smell.

The storm was brewing for at least a day.
Call it a change in barometric pressure
but I sensed the ghost of the guy in 4A
we lost in June. He was in his old room.
The other nurse felt him too.

Happier now, this man.
Kingdom come. *Gone home*
one way people euphemize for *dead*.
Crossed over, they will say, or *passed on*.
I think of it more as simply gone.

But perhaps we get to revisit lost loves,
favourite rooms, best afternoons
when we are *gone*.
A picnic lunch on Hampstead Heath
in 1991, a night out on Camden Town.

That 2 a.m. proposal over a Chianti bottle,
the stolen kiss with a boy I barely knew.
Paris, the spread-out jewellery of her light —
or maybe the spirit gets to do
whatever feels completely right.

Mine will be taking a grand tour
of the United States
in an ivory 1956 Coup de Ville.
No need for gas, rest stop, motel,
just driving, top down, music blowing back

all day and all night: San Francisco
to New York, south to Key West,
through New Orleans and along the Gulf Coast,
the livid dawns, the dusks,
through every shade of white
that the southwest desert glare burns
and the sky turns as I head
inevitably for the Pacific Rim,
the breakers, and the high plunge off the cliffs
to the wild ocean, calling me home to drown.

O Holy Life

We left our flip-flops by the No Lifeguard sign.
The sky was grey and the ocean was grey and white.
There were seals rising up slick black and sinking back down.
We wore the cuttings of the sea goddess's hair
on our feet for ceremonial sandals.
The elk and the deer were there,
they came near from the hills and watched us bow down
before the ocean and the new forest grown up
since the fire, they stared
as we picked up crab shells and searched for eyes.
The seals bobbed their heads out of the lazy swell
and each time though further away
they knew exactly where we were
and we knew exactly where we were.
We were there on the rough sand with the waves
creaming between our toes catching us unawares,
and up in the dunes we lay against a bed of shrubs,
the green springiness and tiny pale yellow flowers
a bed in the dunes for us to rest upon
where the sea was too far away,
and the pines fighting for light and air
having burst out of the fire's heat and ash
were too close to survive, too fertile,
too many — O holy life
that does not know how to stop coming,
how not to flower out of the ash,
that has to give up some of its own
because they crowd too close, too young,
too hopeful, too soon.

Snapshot

Rain beats the blossoms
of the black locust,
beats them down
into a sodden white carpet,
a bride's train dragging
in a narrow street market,
the bride laughing, laughing,
face upturned.

South Beach

I let her drive
on the narrow road down to the beach
between the dunes with their russet ice-plant hair;
she was thirteen, piloting the car with infinite care.

The sea was boiling mad
climbing the beach,
ice-green at the curled-over tops of the waves,
then darker green and churned-up sandy foam.

She stood at the edge
taking video with her phone,
blonde hair blown across her sea-green eyes.
In an instant the gods could decide to snatch her back.

I could no more hold her
than the fine sand,
I could no more keep her safe
than the wind or salty air;

but we stood together there
at the ragged edge of the land
and the churn and rush of the waves merged in a rising choir,
a melody, not sweet, but urgent, uncontrolled;

it sang of me and her,
of the earth that arose, bold,
from the featureless ocean, the hill of the world,
and of all mothers and their wild unpredictable girls;

and the sun god, a phoenix,
alit on the hill where we stood
with her filming the waves, and me
holding on to her in my mind, in my imagination,

so it felt as if
I would always have her near.
And then we walked back up the sandy path to the car
and we got in, and smiled at each other, and I put it in gear.

St Laurence's Ward

When I hugged my glass mother with her slippery slopes
one time before she gave up her ghost
she was pulling at dawn's chains, she was staring
at the children only she could see at the end of the ward.
I looked out the square of pale grey beside her bed
that early morning lightened and whitened, the weeping beeches
still weeping — who could blame them — and the Dublin rain
fitful and slanting out of a circling silver sky.

When I hugged my frail mother, afraid that she would break,
all hell came loose in that moment. I saw her
young and black-haired in her polka-dot dress
the years unravelled from their wooden spool, the frazzle ice
that touched her life all the way back to London's
wartime rubble rimed her elbows and her swollen feet.
Forces of chaos and fate, I begged them
to open the door for her and mercifully send her out.

Sweet Creek Corner

It's time again for a fire poem, a Fall
lyric to the wane, to the dust and ashes
of summer, and the sea change, the rising
order. One afternoon of late August heat
we come along the forest trail, silk soft
brown dust cool beneath our feet, we are floating
and sinking, floating and sinking. Nothing
buoys me like the ceaseless singsong
chatter of her stream, flowing round
Sweet Creek Corner, over the sudden rocks
and into the redwood tunnel, heady scent
of the bays, the two of us in ecstatic embrace
with life, wind behind us always, before me
on the trail butterfly scapulae beneath
her thin T-shirt with the cuff of lace, she asks
if we can sleep out again tonight,
beneath the bear and the hunter and the fish:
I almost wish for the early days,
when it was light before we woke,
but we're on course for September and the shutting down
of freedom, school, the days putting on their geometric
    shapes,
time sorted into boxes. Somehow in these last
good afternoons, through the shaking of the limbs,
the first golden layer of needles and the dancing
I tell her we call dappling, you can see
the ends of the earth, and the rounded hills following
each other over the edge of the cliff.

Fall Back

November again. Isn't this one
always coming around, with its
dead letter days, its footfalls
on wet leaves, its numbed sounds?

There'll be no more laughter now,
and not a lot of happy ever after.
My mother is missing. The stars too,
the stars are not where I left them,
they are not in their constellations.

Through the keyhole of midnight
I have glimpsed the white tiles
of the future, the stark walls
and the uncut shadows. Losing her
to her own life is one thing —

now and then we all take on water,
sink a little lower — but *this little-
understood, misdiagnosed, neurological
disaster*: that this should have
my mother now just seems unsound.

But there it is: the tug of war
between antagonistic muscle groups,
the lost inhibition of wayward
neurons. *Paralysis agitans*. Eventually,
I am told, every movement

must be voluntarily controlled. Today
our creek is suddenly running wild,
following the season's first storm;
walnut leaves, black locust clog the drain
until our road's awash with rain;

the wind soughs in the thickening black.
Last night we fell back, and the clocks
with their one frail extra hour
snatched us out of the jaws of the dark.

Burrow Beach

She really doesn't talk much any more.
Not, I think, because she has nothing to say.
The thoughts are there, but words get in the way.

She has a bed now that makes noise.
The air goes in and out with a quiet thrum,
not like a lullaby that you might hum

to a sleepy child with eyelids growing heavier
but a hospital sound that has invaded her home
like all the other paraphernalia they have on loan

from the health clinic up the hill —
the hoist, commode, chairs with buckles and wheels,
ramps to the front door. All this equipment feels

to me like a crash course in growing old.
I'm now the same age — forty-five —
that she was when her mother died.

So one day all this will be mine:
the blister packs, the overbed table, the pale blue
light of her life washing through

this house like the sea down on the Burrow Beach
that she conjured with her artist's eye from a blank page.
As Thomas exhorted, Rage, rage

against the dying of the light,
and that is what I am doing each day,
raging in my own distilled and private way,

nothing showy — it's not what she would want —
but that doesn't make less bitter or less deep
the sorrow that breaks over me before I sleep.

The Hour

The week slants down towards Friday when we fly;
the night sky tips its bucket of stars towards dawn
and the beach — the beach is sliding into the sea.

The waves are relentless, they just never give up.
While we're flying east they'll still be at it, pawing
the sea wall till it makes its tiny concessions of sand.

Time is stretched out on her hammock of sunshine
and heat, long and lovely. I'm handing her the goods
and she's opening me out like a large flower, a dahlia.

Now we're hurtling down her runway a mile a second,
splitting off from the earth, the cows growing tiny;
the yellow fields where the people make hay look no bigger

than fingernails. Crossing Utah, time takes her hour
payment for flight. We'll get it back in five days,
but I think of it lying quietly in the dark bank vault.

I want it back in the same condition I surrendered it,
laughter round the edges, the chance to rise
above the confines of my life. But what if it were

the hour of my demise, a chance blow, a second
of bad luck? If so, let me stay east, cheating my life
of that borrowed hour, walking free in the fields,

sitting out in the weather, immersed in the warm sea.
Some people come out of the gates smiling.
I promise myself now, that will always be me.

Delta 7123

The heat is streaming off the wing,
the engines climbing into the whine
that will become a scream as we thunder down
the tarmac gathering speed towards noon, towards lift-off,
the crazy possibility that air will bear us.

Leonardo on his deathbed in 1519
said one of his regrets was not to have flown;
and here I am, unremarkable citizen of 2013,
airborne in a silver aeroplane, flying time
half a day, San Francisco to JFK.

The weather is all below us now.
On either side of North America
the waves clamber over each other to make it ashore,
the people stand looking longingly out to sea,
dreamers wholly enveloped in the dream.

But up here it's all perfectly clear.
Wings slice the air. I can see incredibly far
and with the insouciance that comes with flight
I think I'm free to choose
to wander only in the happy rooms of life.

If we crashed now — and you have to admit
the possibility, statistically real — we would go down,
a flurry of lost souls in a shining whirl,
on a beautiful February afternoon
somewhere in Colorado's rocky folds.

When would we be found?
It all looks so innocent, so pristine,
the delicate creases of cliff and ravine,
the steely lakes unruffled, serene.
We might never be found.

If your vest doesn't have a tab
the light will activate automatically in the water.
Federal law should prohibit tampering with the truth.
In the unlikely event of a watery descent
our vests may be supremely suited

to the task for which they were meant
but my husband would be without a wife,
my daughter motherless, poor waif,
and my life flashing before my eyes,
hopefully worth the ticket price.

All dark out there now.
The single light at the end of the wing
a beacon of cheer in the fathomless dark.
Breathe normally and note
that oxygen is flowing.

Is it irrational thirty thousand feet up
to be convinced that nobody gets hurt?
We all make it safely to our destinations,
families waiting with the Welcome Home signs?
Because there it is below —

Manhattan, lit up like a sailor's broad at night.
Sit back, relax, and enjoy the flight.

Shutdown

The day the government shut down
the ocean showed up for work.
They put up some barricades
but waves kept coming in, unfazed.
The toilets were locked
and the barricades went up
to stop the people coming in to the park
but we went early, before they closed
the National Seashore, and I can attest
that the seals and the pelicans
and the small fish and the birds that eat them
kept coming back for more.

The waves were giving it their all,
rending the heart of the beach in two,
throwing their violent weight around
while Congress ran aground;
the rush of foam and fuming toil
of the wind blowing spume back
from the crests as loud as the silence
along the corridors of power,
the sand hot beneath our feet,
the water silvery gold,
the gulls laughing and crying
as we were laughing and crying too.

Pelicans flew as low as they dared.
We reckoned they hadn't heard
that the government was hung —
hoist by its own petard —
that they'd put up some wooden barriers
to stop the tourist cars
from visiting the National Seashore,
while well beneath the roar of the breakers
tearing up the shale

and the keening wail of the gulls
the day was a good day, ungoverned,
lovely, full of miracles.

Dahlias

So many false restarts
but this morning you were at my door,
there was chanting,
there were heavy robes and flowers,
my bones were broken loose
with all the singing.

I hear the wash of the ocean
below the cliffs,
pelican shadows sweep the surf,
the mist blows in but it's under the sun;
above the mist the sun goes on
and on, as it always seems to have done.

It turns out
you can see beauty wherever you look.
It turns out that suffering
is inevitable, ubiquitous, a chance
to go inside the thing, an opportunity
to love.

My spirit steps from stone to stone
along the narrow granite line
to this last one at the cliff edge.
Back among the living in the ordinary afternoon,
grey, chance of rain,
the world is terrible and great again,

the dark between the stars is deep enough
to drown our secret fears, our pain.
Back in my town the sweet falling notes
of mourning doves are a song
to the sun washing out the downy hills
and the pale greeny yellow sky above

and you are there,
layer of harmony on layer,
you are constant as you were before,
you are everything you've always been
and more, let there be no further
lamentation

for it turns out
we can say yes to everything we need
and just in time
our lives can open out with the sun's bounty
like giant flowers — dahlias, splashy,
giddy with promise.

When We Got Home from Paradise

On our way home from Paradise
the hills were quiet, they were
standing still, hair combed,
and in their desiccated colours,
the cows were down in the heat,
the creeks dark shadows,
and just beyond the bend in the long
shimmering road summer was waiting
for her nod, some word, a cue
that things were ready.

When we got home
all the signs were there. The clocks
on fire, the season's calendar
already counting down,
the ticking in the air,
everything so heavy and so light,
and on the answering machine
the doctor's voice. We listened twice,
then it was time to feed
the animals, water all the plants

and clean. It seemed imperative
to clean the house as though a stranger
could drop by at any time. That night
we couldn't lie down, the news
was filling up the bedroom, it was
everywhere, sucking up the air.
Give the doc a call, you said,
as though we could have misconstrued
his words, as though summer
wouldn't one day languidly give way to Fall.

Bluebellies

I dreamed
I married him again
so he wouldn't have to die alone.

Talked to his mother.
She thought he planned it.
He didn't leave a note.

In the end, I hope,
peace: nothingness,
though even nothingness could be too much.

Quiet, then. Snow, maybe.
Desert silence.
Tracks in the snow

showing him
that, even if the bluebellies were long gone
and life were not

a three-ring circus,
a five-alarm fire,
some days worth only

a drive off the road
into the blinding white,
he was not alone.

The Last Word

for Michael (1960-2013)

The summer parties are all thrown,
the summer deaths are done. Fall now,
and the return to work, you know what to do:
rake leaves, journey inward, mask the sad
turn of events with a drive to the coast.

I've come out here alone to find him,
and here he is, alone, where we were once
all set to grow up, grow old together.
I drove by our house on the hill: still the windows,
floors, four walls we tried in vain to make into a home.

The night before we married we stayed up the coast
in a rental place, cavernous, too large for two.
My dress glowed ivory on the back of the bedroom door.
He told me how he couldn't get to sleep
without alcohol any more, and I told him

he could keep doing it or he could stop
and I would love him anyway.
I'd read that somewhere.
Jerry Garcia's wife said that to him.
I thought it sounded brave.

He is beyond help or harm now, beyond reproach,
human suffering, temptation or regret.
He is beyond the shame that clung for so long
to us, colouring every day we called our own.
Fourteen hundred by my reckoning, maybe more.

The trees know how to do it —
let go their leaves when the summer heat
has done them in. Animals get ready

without being told. They know.
Was he frightened beyond belief

as he washed the pills down with his beverage of choice?
Or did he just decide to let it go
and watch with interest as the leaves
massed in drifts by the side of the road?
Did he know?

Do I? Do I have the first idea what it's all for?
Three weeks now, nobody bore his weight
down an aisle, sent flowers.
This is his eulogy: these few words on a beach
where we once whiled away the hours.

What were all those words we said? Love whispers,
vows, bitter retorts. Syllables carved in the wet sand
and, while the darkness lingered, blown over by the dry.
I've come here to say it at last
as you can into the crashing of the waves

and the ocean wind that snatches the little word
and takes it spinning and fluttering
through the ice blue of the air.
Au revoir would be dishonest.
It has to be *goodbye*.

On Not Scattering Michael's Ashes in Death Valley

I didn't need the ashes
nor the desert's sackcloth.
I didn't need to scatter anything
to understand we suffer so we learn.
That I have long known. Back then
it was all learning.

The parking place at the top of Ottinger Hill
was dark colours, so I moved on.
Mount Vision was all greens,
wild iris blue and poppy gold.
The birds were celebrating *a capella.*
I hoped that he could hear them.

We hiked this mountain sixteen years ago,
a cold day the winter I returned to him.
We started out together but I turned back,
drove home and waited in the quiet.
He came after dark having had it out
with his demons on the mountaintop,
the wildness in him trying to outsmart,
outmanoeuvre the savagery in them.
It wasn't clear who'd won.

Drake's Bay and the Estero looked flat
and far away from the mountain's height.
On the Tomales side, hills leaned gently
into gentle hills in the watercolour light.
At Drake's Beach the restaurant was gone,
a park ranger cut the grass around the poppy tufts,
the ocean spoke in a soft voice,
said I didn't need to wait here any more
and gave me what I had been looking for.

The clock said eleven at last.
Time turned over from the past
into the boundless, new, never-before-encountered
now. The sand was warm,
the rocks warm, the sun came out:
surely a benediction of some sort.

I felt his spirit near, awake in freedom,
exulting in the small birds' incantations.
He seemed to wave me off as if he was sure
he didn't need anything from me any more,
and the day was young, lovely like a girl
just awakening to her power.

Sleep Train

Night after night
snake of a train
meanders through valleys
and coastal towns.
I make my way
through the sleeping cars;
fluttering in the breeze,
the late night hours.
Happiness is a choice
that night after night
awake on a train
through the somnolent towns
with their unsung hymns
I choose.

Again and again
I don't make the call,
the sick get sicker
and the dead remain dead.
Summer is slipping,
the moon is half empty,
the moon is half full.
I make the call.
Over the static
we say our things:
you were right to leave,
I'm this, you're that,
the landscape we travelled
was ugly and flat.

Afternoons
at the reservoir
the water is low,
slate grey, disgruntled
by a temperamental breeze;

along the road my car
drove through a flurry
of gold leaves.
Had there been sunlight
they would have shone. As it was
they were here, they're gone
between the old growth
and the rings of time.

The truth is this,
as far as I see:
intimacy
is a well-meant lie
and so is control
and so is joy.
We are each alone
on the sleeping train
night after night
through the broken towns,
the good gone to ground
and the dark gone awry;
again and again
lie within lie.

You could end it there,
that would be okay
but night follows day
follows night follows day.
The view out the window
may be ugly and flat
but you can't see beyond
the next bend in the track.
The moon is a lantern
that breaks on my skin;
out at the ocean

wave after wave,
giving up is cowardly,
going on is brave.

Things fall apart,
new things are made.
Giving up is cowardly,
going on is brave.

Emergency Chocolate

Our house is falling into the sea.
The slide, we saw it coming, is irreversible.
The living room is gone, we cannot live in it
any more. Sea water enters through
our back door, kitchen soon to be submerged,
roof caved in beyond repair. Barnacles reside
where we once laid our heads
on goose-down pillows, feather beds.

We have emergency chocolate,
pots and pans, a few blankets
for the long winter nights on the front lawn.
Or maybe we will move a little inland
as the sand and detritus
take over our home,
as the sea foam floats around our dining room
with the pull-out table seating twelve.

And we are not alone.
All our neighbours on this stretch of the shore —
the tides have inched inside
their living rooms, entered without knocking
at their front door;
none of us have houses any more;
and the worst of it is
some of them don't even have emergency chocolate.

Ceanothus Celestial Blue

Came out to see the ocean
but the rain had other plans,
drawing veils across the forested hills.

Coffeeberry came back after the fire,
ceanothus, coyote brush,
resin-sealed bishop pine cones

that would have been such
closely guarded secrets
opened in the heat, their juice

spilling out with the smoke.
This is what I do
when I set myself loose:

I drive out through the state
to Mothers of the Night,
Musette and Drums, listening hard

to the quiet between songs.
It's not much, just snatches,
bursts of chatter over the static

but it's the best the dead can manage.
It's Fall, they say, *and there's
no stopping it now is there?*

What It's All For

Hour by hour the contours of the beach can shift,
something that seems as solid as a dune
is not. Nothing permanent, then, is that it?
Maybe the search for a point is what it's all about.
The waves so terrifying, the crystal blue of the sky,
the wind combing the dune grasses — maybe that's the why.
Happiness, in spite of it all: the agony, the wondering,
and the doubt. The sand is hot beneath my feet,
that's what it's all about, the feel of hot sand
as I wander dreamily back towards my car. Happiness
has meaning, the path meandering over the hill
through the ice plant to the asphalt
of the parking lot — joy, delight. It always has, always will.

What Just Happened?

'What just happened,
and where does it leave us?'
'Same place,' he said, but that's not true.
We are in a different place now,
this place is new, we've never been here
before, the air's a different shape,
no colours I've ever seen, the view
has shifted, and the ground
is shifting too, not so easy
to walk around without a fall.
Still, what is there to risk
in this endeavour if not all?

Miners are trained when things go wrong
to lie on the ground, breathe slow
and shallow, wait until the light breaks at last
through a chink and they are found.
Sometimes behind their self-made barricades
they lie there breathing low
until their lives rise up and float around
above them, no colours they've ever seen,
memories shedding light in the coal-dust gloom,
making room for what's to come.

We've been lying here for quite some time.
I'm wondering when we'll be done
with all the shallow breathing
and the oxygen conservation.

Ice Diamond

Glaciers breathe, they move.
Snow stacks up to ice in the upper altitudes,
snow melts down near the snout.
The glacier breathes in in winter,
in summer it breathes out.

When enough ice weighs down on it
ice itself can flow.
We know the melted ones by their moraines —
the piles of rubble they ploughed
when real ice ran through their veins.

Twenty thousand years ago
Switzerland was a sea of ice,
only the high Alp peaks poked out —
the glaciers breathed in in winter,
in summer they breathed out.

In the 1800s, the Little Ice Age,
ice crags suffused with blue light
in a daguerreotype of moraines,
the piles of rubble left by the old monsters
when real ice ran through their veins.

If we weren't changing it now ourselves,
if Nature were still in control,
we'd be due for another ice age soon.
Destined to melt, an enormous chunk of Icelandic ice
glows in the light of the moon.

As the world warms a glacier seeks balance,
an altitude and a mass
at which snow added above equals ice melted below.
On a wintry Icelandic beach the ice diamond
breathes hard in the blue moon's glow.

Universal Laws

Later than midnight, almost early, I'm out driving.
I pass all the houses and the people who live in them
with their layered and overlapping lives, their quiet abiding
by the universal laws — that increasing atomic weight
drives the periodicity of the table, that love is an art
if you do it well, that eventually
potassium moves down its concentration gradient
and diffuses out of the cell.

The road ribbons on, endless and straight
between dry mountains and hot plains.
Over the border it's supposed to be sudden Oregon green
but I've driven all night and in the glow of the infant dawn
the country looks the same — ninety-two natural elements,
a gorgeous blend of soil, cool air, and birds above
the plates shifting and vying far below for purchase,
under all the slaking the same thirst.

At a motel on Highway 99
in the veiled dance between sleeping and waking
I catch glimpses of who I might have been in former lives,
the morning offers up her crickets and her winged insects
humming against the turned-down lamps.
Maybe I was an Emperor who died surrounded by his wives,
but I think it was often hunger, I think I sometimes drowned,
and now my life is underpinned by everything I've learned:

layers of music, life upon life, and still I'm unprepared
for the crazy joy, the blur of things, the longing,
the size of the waves once I'm in them, the heights
I'm brought to, the visibility up here, longevity
of human kindness across time: that we are all one consciousness,
that god has left the building, yet we continue to expand
in the sleek pearly white low-power happiness of being,
long after all the stars have died.

Ashes, Phoenix

Now that I'm done,
now that the last appeal has been wrung
from me, the first dawn can come
again in all its innocence, its cold
comfort and splendour, so reliable,
so familiar, so aloof.

Beneath the surface,
ready to breach, kings of the deep
sound the alarm, they break open the ocean
and crash back down, splayed tails
churning foam, and the waves in return
make their sound

like the trees,
and the trees make their sound like the waves,
and I'm ready to consider all harm,
all futures or no future at all,
so many more have died than are still alive.
I see them everywhere

and they are lost
in the past, they are quivering
in and out of existence, and it's so much darker
where they are than I'd imagined, so much warmer,
more galaxies than there are stars in the Milky Way,
more worlds, more dark matter

counteracting the pull
of the light, dark energy driving things apart,
and I'm ready to look up, put words
on the nameless longing, listen to the dawn
telling me the nature of my life, calling it
ashes, phoenix.

Big Dry

At the peak of the [Australian] drought it became very apparent that the environment doesn't lie.
— Mike Young, Professor, University of Adelaide

Big black buzzard just flew overhead,
wings doing that slow thrumming,
flock of Canada geese on the far shore
making plans for their flight south;
now they are coming in delegations
of four and five, the low wings
over the water, the mournful chanting,
skidding down into what little is left
of our reservoir, the south end of which
is a new wetland lush with grasses,
a meadow that shouldn't be there,
the old road with the stone bridge
that is only revealed when the rains
don't come and still don't come.

Big Dry, the Australians called
their ten-year thirst, their decade of drought,
but they figured out, once the land
warned them and taught them,
how to stretch the water, make it last,
reform the allocation system,
charge for it, make all wastage hurt.

It's not that the geese are asking anything
of their lone observer on the muddy shore.
Just that I can't offer them anything,
no promises, no casual assurances
that next Thursday the forecast says
ninety percent chance of rain, moving into
the weekend. Snow at higher elevations.

This was their refuge, their wild home.
Why should they, how could they know
that wildfire season is now
two months longer than thirty years ago —
the burns more frequent, more intense?
Wildfires in January; or that Shasta Lake
shrank so much this spring it disgorged
its secrets: tree stumps submerged
in 1945? What they need is the wingtip vortex
of the bird in front to reduce the drag
in the V formation, enough water
to survive and, high in the Sierras,
the air to tremble and shimmer
with the promise of snow.

Famine Cottages

The horses move across the top of the hill,
the water's still as stone below.
If I had to let it all in
to the places where I feel at home
I'm certain it would take me down,
I would be undone,
I'd drown.

As it is there is little purchase
on my surface. Few ways in.
The trees send up their prayers for rain,
the hills colour up at the mention of spring.
This year I have been more than half my life
elsewhere. For so long I have been other,
insular, a foreigner with the buried idiom.

Across the reservoir deer paths lace the hillside.
In my pocket two stones and a shell
from the beach below the famine cottages
at Rossohan. We used to row there in a skiff.
Last night the driving California rain
drove home to me
how far away

are those beaches where we played as kids: Dog's Bay,
Inch, Cahirciveen, the dry stone walls squaring off
their handkerchiefs of land. New Year's Eve
1993, I flew across
an ocean and six thousand miles to be
where I am now,
and this is how

I've lived my adult life — away from
my original home, in a new place
with new people, an about face

from all I'd known. This is what I chose —
the airport departures halls, the agonized farewells,
and now these hills, my northern moon,
my pre-dawn birds.

Coyotes

Gravity cannot account for falling in love.
— Albert Einstein

2 a.m. and the coyotes start
with their howls of victory and despair.
I'm seeing it everywhere: the keys in their jar,
the bird that flew up unhurt this morning
from beneath the car, an insect's gauzy wings
against the lamp — we live as though these things
and how the day went
constitute the only way things are.

When I make these journeys
back to the country of my birth
it feels like flying into the old
territory of my roadless self, my history.
Days before I board the plane
I start to shed the layers of it all
like parchment wrappings, then I step
into empty time in the departures hall.

They board the infants, then first class,
then the rest of us. Rush of take-off,
the brilliant sky and the clouds.
Because of the uncertainty principle
space is never empty; because of supergravity
and supersymmetry we have unified theories
of everything, including the seven unplanned
curled up other dimensions I can't fully understand.

But I have formed my own slender theory
of quantum uncertainty, cradled up here
in the stratosphere by the laws of nature
and the four forces: if all of existence
is just patterns of vibrations without width or height,

end or start, then what connects us
must be the wildness that runs riot
in the clamorous chambers of the heart.

In the big past it's understood
that stars burned through their hydrogen till they collapsed,
beryllium fused with helium before it could decay
to form a stable carbon isotope
which is how I'm sitting here today,
unruly conduit from heart to page
for all the sudden joy, the human hurt
and sorrow, laughter, love, and rage

that makes us undertake
these solo expeditions into the territory.
There isn't any map.
You have to be the architect of your life,
the poet of it, hunger for what the future holds,
face the inevitable, the unknown and, like the coyotes,
pound down the double doors of the night and come out
fires blazing, eyes wide open, heart alight.